STAND OUT THE TED WAY:

Be Seen & Grow Your Business

Dolores Hirschmann, ACC, CPCC

Stand Out the TED Way
Be Seen & Grow Your Business

Published by:
Dolores Hirschmann
www.mastersinclarity.com
Copyright © 2018, Dolores Hirschmann
All Rights Reserved.

Published in the United States of America I No parts of this publication may be reproduced without correct attribution to the author of this book.

ISBN - 9781729515211

Here's What's Inside...

- Introduction 9

- Why Do Small Businesses Entrepreneurs Struggle with Attracting Clients? 13

- What do TED talks have to do with Sales & Growing a Business? 17

- The Mistakes Businesses Make 22

- The Difference between a Sales Funnel & a Trust Funnel 26

- "Standing Out the TED Way" works for all kinds of Businesses 31

- Applying this Method to Your Business. 35

Testimonials

"Dolores helped me get clear on the title and topic of my talk. In helping me with my TEDx Talk she was able to see the real essence of what I do and I'm incredibly grateful. Thank you Dolores" – Fabienne Fredrickson, Founder of Boldheart; Business Mentor; Speaker; Author & TEDx Speaker

*"I found working with Dolores incredibly helpful! From our very first meeting to our last call before my TEDx talk, she gave me inspirational ideas, specific strategies, compassionate criticism, and heartfelt help. In our initial meeting, she helped me filter through my treasure chest of ideas to find the diamond in the rough. Through each meeting, she helped me polish the diamond and smooth out the rough edges. I really appreciated her specific feedback on the various elements of my talk --- intro, body, photos, and conclusion. She was also helpful in reviewing my presentation style. I greatly

appreciated her ability to effectively work with me in various formats: in person, on the phone, through email and written feedback, and reviewing my videos of my talk. Overall, giving my TEDx talk was a life changing experience. It allowed me an opportunity to go inside myself to explore a topic and then share it with the world. My greatest highlight was having my daughters sit in the TEDx audience and hear my talk first hand. Thank you for helping me with such a gift of connection. I am so grateful." – Andy Goldfarb, Co Founder & Executive Managing Director Globespan Capital Partners

"My conversations with Dolores when I was in the development phase of my TEDx talk were incredibly helpful. While I provided a laundry list of things I was hoping to cover in my talk, Dolores was able to concentrate my thoughts and help me to focus on the main idea and the most powerful theme of my thoughts. Dolores was tremendously helpful in clarifying the main ideas in my talk. She also provided great tips as far as storytelling and actual delivery of my talk. Agreeing to *speak to a crowd of over 700 can be daunting. Dolores was very supportive and encouraging and validated the direction and importance of what I hoped to talk about. Her feedback was insightful and thoughtful and very helpful, particularly at a moment when I felt a bit 'stuck.' Her thoughts helped me to move forward in my drafting."* – Lauren Prestileo, Series Producer WGBH and TEDx speaker

"Working together allowed me to hone in on what it was I was trying to say or the message I wanted to have people leave with. I found the handouts on formulating a TEDx talk also to be very helpful. Working together definitely helped me clarify my ideas, the flow of the talk, and time management of the whole process. I would say that working with Dolores was a supportive and loving experience, solid advice and coaching, always with optimism and love." – Zoe Hansen-DiBello, TEDx speaker

"Your coaching was superb! I had trouble finding comfort in sharing my story; it felt at first as if the focus was on me, while the

focus should have been in trying to help others. You helped me see the benefits of letting the crowd relate to my experiences, and it made all the difference. Before your coaching, my idea worth spreading was fully developed, but the de- livery was still very much disorganized. After your coaching, I had flow and found comfort in my wording, my idea, and impact, and I had a stronger delivery. Dolores is caring, strategic in providing feedback, and FUN! Whether or not you feel you need coaching, you should book at least one session with Dolores and let her open your mind with insights gained from her unique experiences in dealing with talented speakers." – Joshua Encarnacion, TEDx speaker

"I loved working with Dolores. My project has benefited substantially from our work together. Our sessions have helped me to gain new insights on my own personality, gain clarity on my message to my different target groups and motivated me to express my own personality more in my work. I am now a more confident and effective communicator. And it has paid off in my work allowing me to reach my professional goals. Dolores has an exceptional personality. She is excited to work with. She will bring out the best in you." – Maximilian Weidl, Founder MED Leaders, Entrepreneur

"Before I started with Dolores I had multiple ideas and absolutely NO action on any of them. I felt despair at times that nothing I wanted to do could happen because I didn't know where to start. Dolores walked me through the most important strategies to help me prioritize and think clearly about my business and how it fits in with my current lifestyle. I am much more focused and willing to let go of what doesn't work, and excited to try out so many new things one step at a time! With Dolores's coaching I now have new bold ideas, messaging strategies, and consistency. Dolores is the go to person to get re-energized, inspired, and motivated to actually get shit done. Don't use her if you don't want results!" – Lea Berry, Founder LeaBerryCoaching

Introduction

As a TEDx Organizer, I am passionate about IDEAS. Every year, we curate from hundreds of speakers who are looking to stand out, through the application process and get selected to speak. Many of these speakers have great IDEAS that they want to share with the world but most of them don't stand out from their competition. I see this problem in my work as well. I work with entrepreneurs and small businesses that are looking to attract their ideal clients and grow their businesses but they fail when trying to stand out, to be seen, to reach their market and close the sale. Being seen and attracting clients is the blood of ANY business. No customers, no business. Period. It does not matter how good your product or service is, if nobody is buying it then you are not really "in" business!

This is a very REAL problem and one that can paralyze any early stage entrepreneur or small business owner. I have been in that place as well. When I first launched my coaching practice, looking to be a life coach at the time, I struggled with finding my place and finding the way I could stand out and position my services in a unique way. It took me years to realize what was special about my company and to communicate this effectively. For years, I felt like I was doing "busy" work with no real results. Nothing I did seem to generate the outcome I wanted. It made me feel overwhelmed, frustrated, full of self-doubt and in fear of failing. It felt like everyone else had it right, but I didn't.

Only when I was able to clearly position myself in the marketplace and stand out in my unique way, did my business gain the momentum and traction that has allowed me to double my revenue, year to year, reaching multiple six figures in my third year in business! Growth happened quickly when I got my ducks in a row when I began to STAND OUT!

This lack of clarity in your brand, your message and your unique value proposition (I call it your CORE IDEA) is what stops entrepreneurs, small businesses, and professionals from growing a successful business that feels abundant, aligned and fun! It prevents them from reaching a larger market and serving their clients with their products and services.

One client I helped with my program is a successful executive coach with an impressive corporate career who was growing his business in the corporate world. He came to me ready to grow his business but unsure of how to position his company to attract his ideal client.

As we began the exploration phase, he became clearer about what was unique about his company and how he was different from other professionals in his industry. He began to see his driver, the heart of his company, what his company stands for. This clarity not only led him to position his brand and his message in a unique way, but it has also impacted the products and services he offers to offer more targeted, solution based services that are serving his clients at a higher level. His company doubles year to year and now having built a successful team, he is able to spend most of the time doing what he loves the most and taking time for his personal life!

I hope this book inspires you to seek the clarity you need to **Stand Out and Grow Your Business.** My hope is that understanding what is behind the work that you do will allow you to communicate your message from a place of higher vision, purpose, and passion and thus engaging with your ideal client and growing your business.

Enjoy the book! In Clarity!

Why Do Small Businesses & Entrepreneurs Struggle with Attracting Clients?

Entrepreneurs and Small Businesses tend to focus on sharing information about their products and services, where you can purchase from them, what packages they offer, the details of their products and where to find them, etc.

Just like any other business in their industry, they are trying to close a sale. Attract a client and sell something. They are operating from a mindset of "winning the sale".

Their attention is placed 100% on closing that sale.

What if I were to say that closing the sale is a "CONSEQUENCE" not the goal of top salespeople? That getting a client to purchase from you is a result of building a trust- based relationship with your prospective clients? Indeed, Standing Out the TED way requires that you move from the place of selling to the place of attracting. That you engage with your audience from a mindset of "adding value" and caring for your market in such a way that you a are willing to take a stand for them by serving them at your highest level.

In an article written by Eric Wagner, for Forbes Magazine, Wagner identifies 5 reasons for small businesses and entrepreneurs failing to reach their potential. The first 3 are directly related to the problems of Standing Out and Being Seen, the last 2 are a VERY REAL concern and while it's not the focus of this book, it's one of the key elements I work with my clients:

- Reason #1: Not really in touch with customers through deep dialogue.

- Reason #2: No real differentiation in the market

- Reason #3: Failure to communicate value propositions in clear, concise and compelling fashion.

- Reason #4: Leadership breakdown at the top

- Reason #5: Inability to nail a profitable business model with proven revenue streams. According to the Bureau of Labor Statistics, about one-third of businesses will fail within the first 2 years and only 50% of businesses will survive at least 5 years.

Is your business part of that one third?

So, in order to build a trust-based relationship and engage with your market from a place of adding value, you first need to get to know them!

Let's Explore

How well you know your ideal client by answering these questions: What is your client's struggle? What problem are they trying to solve?

What does this "problem" or pain make them feel?

What do TED talks have to do with Sales & Growing a Business?

Let me begin by explaining what TED is. TED is a non-profit organization based in New York City. It's where TED talks started. It started as a small, private conference in California, and has evolved over time. After a few years, it was decided to share the videos of people's talks for free online on TED.com. TED stands for Technology, Entertainment, and Design. These were the three spaces that TED speakers explored. Nowadays, you can probably find a TED talk on almost ANY topic.

TED's tagline is "IDEAS worth spreading". This is what called my attention to the organization in the first place. The opportunity to engage in a conversation about IDEAS was not only intriguing to me; it was exactly aligned with my passion!

TED speakers have one goal; to inspire you to engage with their IDEAS. You could say these speakers are IDEA salespeople... do you see where I'm going with this?

These speakers are passionate and committed to their ideas and they are taking a stand by speaking up for them.

If you've never watched any of these talks, go to www.TED.com to find millions of them.

TED Talks have a very concrete format:

- They need to be delivered in under 18 minutes
- They are to share one MAIN IDEA
- They are supposed to INSPIRE you to take action
- They are concrete and concise enough that you will remember them
- They are designed to have an emotional experience that engages both your heart and your mind TED Speakers and TED talks have grown exponentially in the last 10 years for the simple reason that audiences don't want to just learn something new. They want to be inspired, they want to be activated, and they want to be moved

to action. This happens when the speaker, the person teaching or delivering the information, actually connects and engages with their audience. And that is where TED and TED talks become relevant in the world of business.

In today's crowded world, brands that can engage and inspire their markets and prospective clients, are getting the attention, the following and the market share. Why? Simply because the market resonates with their message, the market feels that the brand understands their need and that they are taking a stand for them.

Companies that do this successfully are connecting emotionally and meeting their market where they are. Instead of pushing content and information down their throats (what it's known as PUSH marketing), they are engaging with their market's emotions and triggering their curiosity, inviting them to engage, to PULL, to ask for more. They are taking their prospective clients on a journey through which the potential client feels safe and validated and through which the potential client begins the trust relationship needed to purchase the company's product or service. Think about brands such as:

- Apple
- Amazon
- Life is Good
- Chobani
- Tesla
- TOMS Shoes

There's a great talk, by TED Speaker Simon Sinek, "How Great Leaders Inspire Action", which talks about the concept of emotionally connecting with a brand.

Let's Explore

What do your potential clients dream of? Write down what is your IDEAL CLIENT's dream. Use as many words as you need to describe that IDEAL solution. The IDEAL world that they aspire to.

What would it look like to inspire your

market? Write down 5 words or statements you can use to INSPIRE your market?

Mistakes Businesses Make When Trying to Get Seen & Build Trust

We are all in agreement that businesses need to be seen in order to grow, but being seen is just the beginning of building a trust-based relationship.

Let's understand the top 10 mistakes companies do when looking to Stand Out.

1. THEY ARE NOT CLEAR ON THEIR AUDIENCE: We've already talked about this. It's hard to have a conversation not knowing who you are really talking to

2. THEY FISH IN THE WRONG POND: Knowing who your ideal client comes first, then you need to be really clear where they gather. Where you can find them?

3. THEY FOCUS ON THE PRODUCT, NOT THE OUTCOME: Customers want to know you will solve their problem, they are less concerned about HOW you will accomplish that. This comes later in the engagement.

4. THEY LACK CONSISTENCY: Connecting

with your audience sporadically in newsletters, social media platforms, blogs, or other outlets is like trying to build a dating relationship and only calling when you feel like it... it will not likely lead anywhere

5. THEIR MESSAGE IS NOT CLEAR: There is no through-line in their messaging. It lacks cohesiveness.

6. THEY ARE SPREAD TOO THIN: In an effort to be seen, they are showing up on multiple platforms not really building a presence in any.

7. THEY FAIL TO ENGAGE: Being seen is the first step of engagement, with technology allowing audiences to openly interact with their audience, companies need to be highly responsive in engaging with comments and messages on digital platforms.

8. THEY MISS THE HUMAN TOUCH: Showing up in person, offering customers an opportunity for a more in person connection can go a long way towards establishing a trust-based relationship.

9. THEY MISS THE FEEDBACK LOOP: **At the end of the day, visibility and building trust is the first part of the sales process. Each strategy, each action needs to be measured and analyze effectiveness. We can't improve what we don't measure.**

10. THEY FAIL TO PLAN: **A well known saying states that failing to plan is planning to fail. Your visibility strategy needs to be intentional, thought out and implemented in an organized way.**

Let's Explore

Which of these 10 MISTAKES resonates with your company? Write it down:

What is one action you can take?

The Difference Between a Sales Funnel & a Trust Funnel

Sales funnel refers to the process that brings a customer from discovering your product or service to completing a purchase. This framework is useful because by dissecting and better understanding the model, marketers and salespeople can more effectively map their strategies and influence outcomes.

This process is focused 100% on doing what we need to do to move the customer through the process.

This is the backbone of any company.

Without a clear process from discovery to sale, it is almost impossible to build a solid, sustainable growing business.

But what if we were to slightly shift the way we think about this process and instead of thinking it as sales process we think of it as a TRUST FUNNEL – a process of consistently building a trustworthy relationship with your ideal client. Let's be clear, the outcome is the same, to close the sale, but by taking this perspective, we have more room for tapping into the human side, into the emotional experience of our market and focus on adding value, in every step creating a sense of safety and trust.

"Our study concludes that this is the percentage of our customers who will buy from us without any effort whatsoever on our part."

Let's Break Down this Process:

1. TOP OF THE FUNNEL: **Decide what visibility actions you will take in a consistent way. Public Speaking, Digital Ads, Partners, Website, Social media, networking, etc.**

2. ENGAGEMENT: **Now that you've been seen, how do you engage? Some great strategies include Online webinars, videos, live Q & A, In person workshops, information sessions, public appearances, Newsletters, online commenting and conversations.**

3. INITIAL PRODUCT MIX: Just like dating, you don't typically go from a "getting to know you date" to marriage... unless you are my husband, who decided to propose after our first blind date ;-)! So, what does that second and third date look like? What product or service can you offer your market that feels safe, for this level of trust?

4. HIGHER COMMITMENT PRODUCT: Now that we know each other, you have your customer's trust, what is the next step?. What is the next product or service they will say yes to now that they know you are the one to solve their pain point?

5. RETENTION: This is the most important part of the TRUST FUNNEL-- The moment your customer becomes a loyal, returning, referring customer. Once you get to this point, your customer is not just someone you can count on for recurring revenue; they also become your best "FREE SALES FORCE" – the drivers of effective word of mouth!

Let's Explore

What is your TOP OF THE FUNNEL strategies? List your top 3 and how consistent you are with these:

What is your INITIAL PRODUCT MIX? Write it down:

Every Business can benefit from Standing Out the TED Way ... especially if you are in a service-based business!

This methodology will show you:

- How to get daily requests for your work.
- How to get people tagging you online and referring you work.
- How to create communities that follow for you.
- How to move toward passive income.
- How to close the room after a speaking engagement.
- How to clarify what makes you "STAND OUT" right now and use it succesfully.
- How to be "powerfully confident."
- How to create consistent cash flow.
- How to create original, compelling content consistently.
- How to take assertive clear action on a daily basis

Here's the Method we use ... THE IDEA METHOD:

• GET CLEAR ON YOUR CORE IDEA:

Just like TED speakers need to begin by clarifying their core IDEA before they write their talk, you need to get REALLY clear on your UNIQUE VALUE PROPOSITION – you need to lead with talking about what you STAND for not what you DO. This will become the foundation of all your messaging.

• FIND YOUR UNIQUE VOICE: I say this all the time when coaching TEDx speakers. Your IDEA is likely to NOT be unique, there are probably a lot of speakers talking about this, so why are you different? It's the same for your company. You are likely one of many professionals offering this product or service, why are you different?

- **FIND YOUR POND:** Identify where your IDEAL client lives. Where do they gather, where do they hang out, where do they connect? Find the pond, hang out there!

- **FOCUS ON RESULTS:** At the end of the day, your ideal client wants their problem solved. Be impeccable in delivering products and services that work and showcase your success stories.

- **BE HUMAN:** It doesn't matter if you are a solopreneur just starting or a large multi-million dollar business, behind every post, newsletter or ad is a human being, make sure you never forget the human touch.

Let's Explore

YOUR CORE IDEA. How clear are you on your CORE IDEA behind your products and services? Can you state it in a short sentence? Try it here:

Your Unique Voice

What is different about your company? – Let me give you an example, I'm a business and communications coach, how am I different? I have business credentials (from business school), coaching credentials (ICF accredited) and I have spent 7 years working as TEDx organizer and involved with TED conferences. While there are many business and communication coaches out there, few combine these skills and experiences. Oh and I forgot to say, I'm from Argentina, and I coach both in English and Spanish AND our clients not only get coaching, they get IMPLEMENTATION too as our programs INCLUDE dedicated VA (Virtual Assistant) to get your work done! Now you try. Why is your company different from your competition?

Applying The IDEA Method to Your Business

This is Masters *in* Clarity's proprietary method designed to guide business owners through a series of steps that result in clarifying and implementing a growth strategy that helps them stand out and grow their business. I call these the "must-have layers of clarity" that your business needs to grow in a sustainable and profitable way.

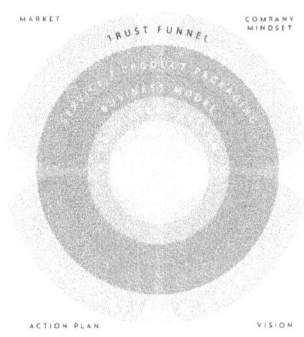

The 5 Core Clarity Layers

1. **YOUR IDEA** - Get clear on the CORE IDEA, CORE VALUE PROPOSITION! At the end of the day, you have one message to share; what is it?

2. **PROPRIETARY SYSTEM** - Put that idea to work! What is the unique proprietary "recipe" that allows you to bring your idea to the marketplace?

3. BUSINESS MODEL - What is the ideal business model in which you will market your idea?

4. SERVICE/PRODUCT PACKAGING - What is the most efficient way to package your products and services within the business model defined?

5. TRUST FUNNEL - How are you going to bring these products and services to the market in a way that feels authentic, makes you stand out, and establishes a trust-based connection with your desired market?

The 4 Supporting Clarity Layers

1. MARKET - Who do you want to be a hero to?
2. VISION - What does impact look like?
3. COMPANY MINDSET - What does your company culture look like? How do you empower and lean into possibility and opportunity?
4. ACTION PLAN - What does "action" look like at each step of the way?

Now What?

If you're ready to stand out the TED way:

Visit us at http://mastersinclarity.com and select <u>START HERE</u> to learn more and book a FREE CLARITY SESSION where we will tell you more about our programs or email us directly at team@mastersinclarity.com